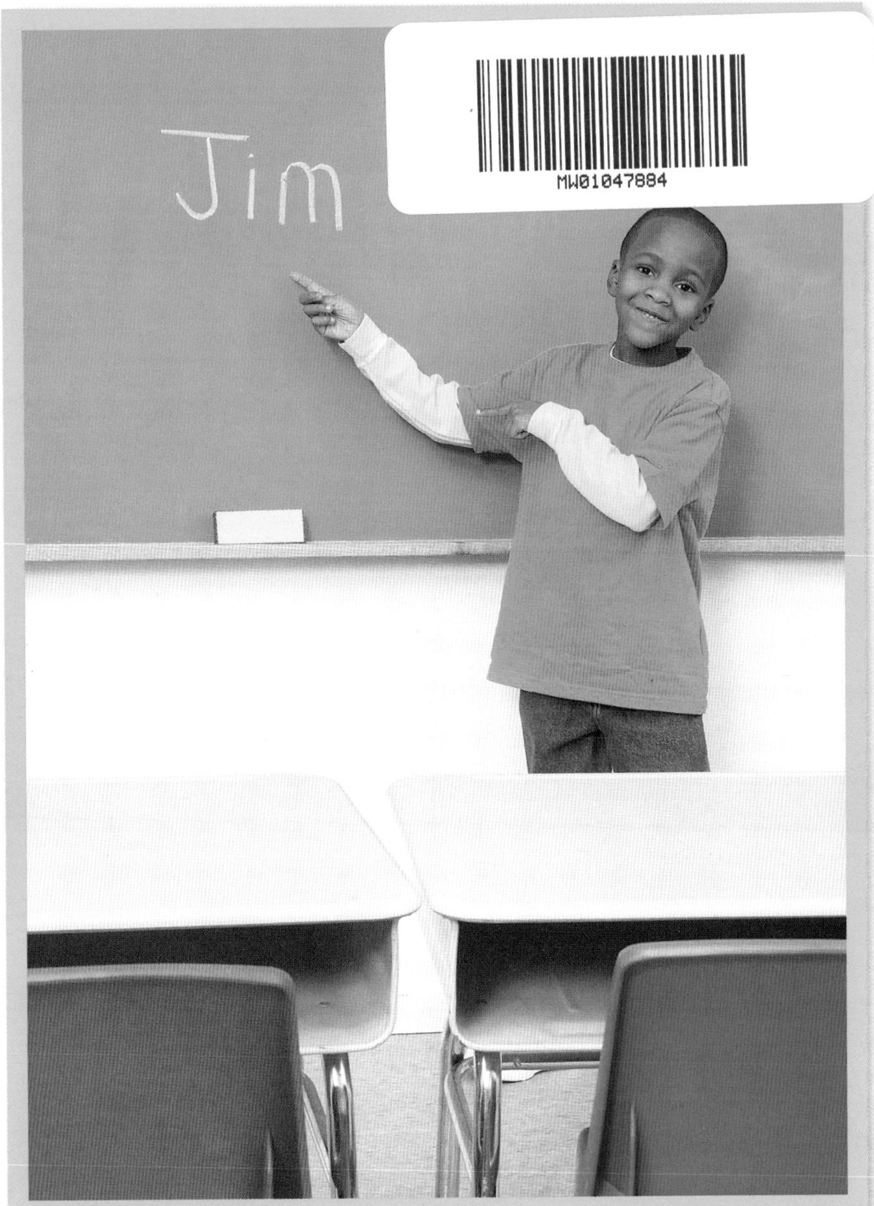

I can read this name.

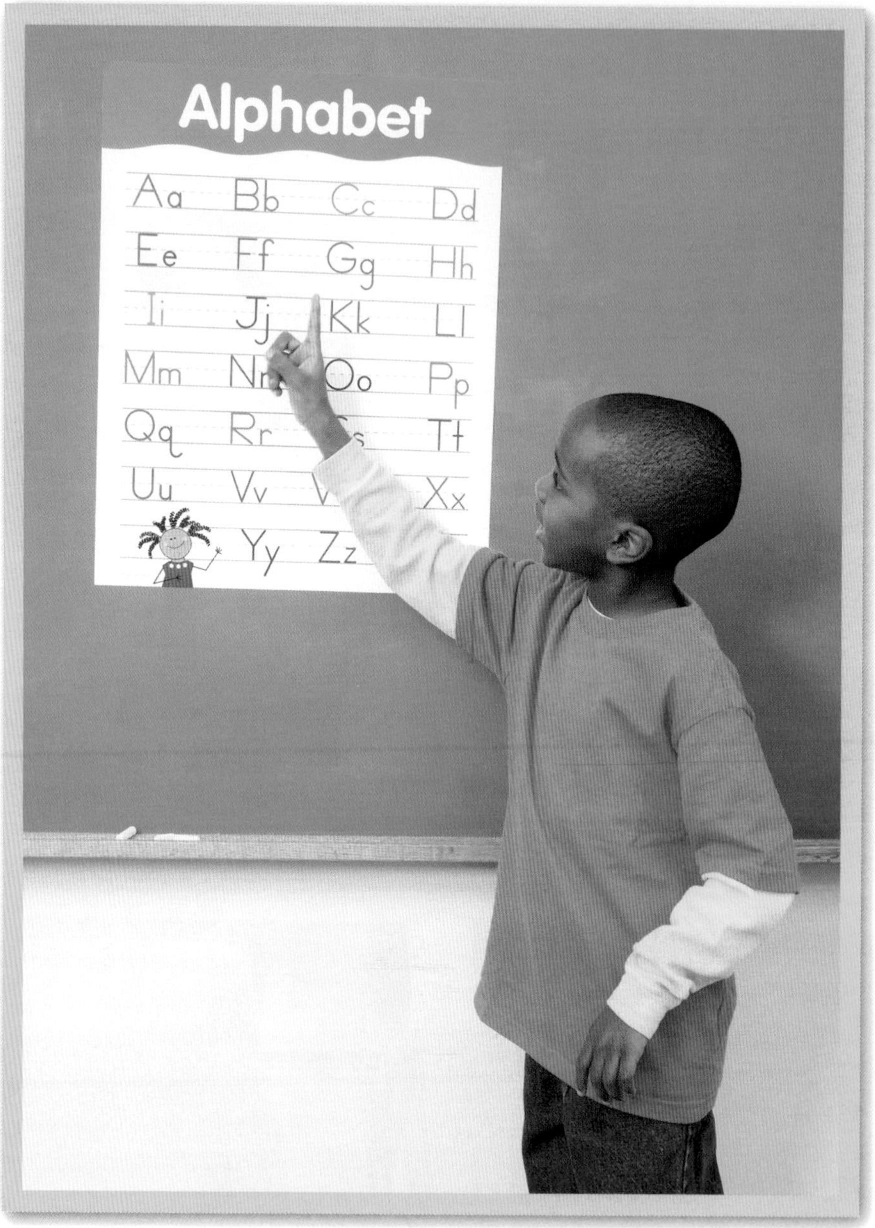

I can read this letter.

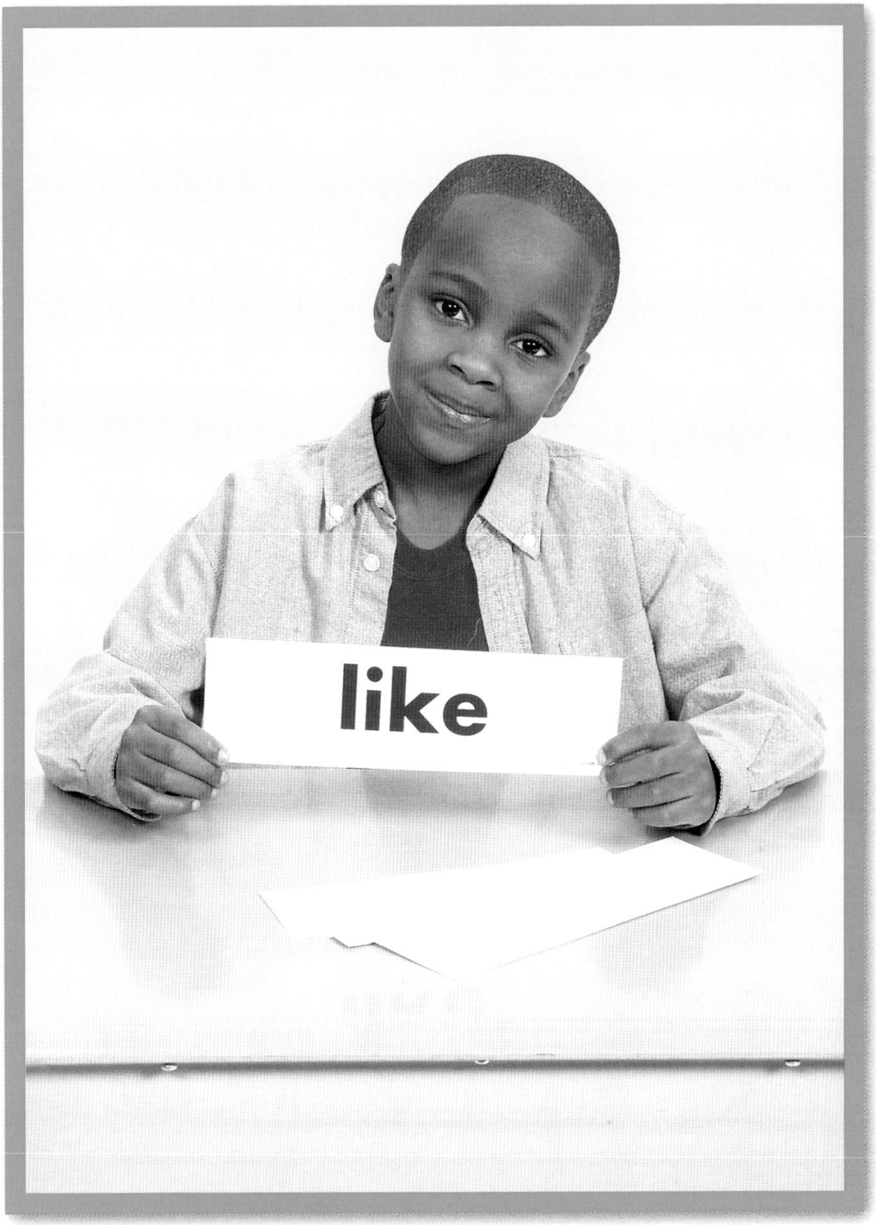

I can read this word.

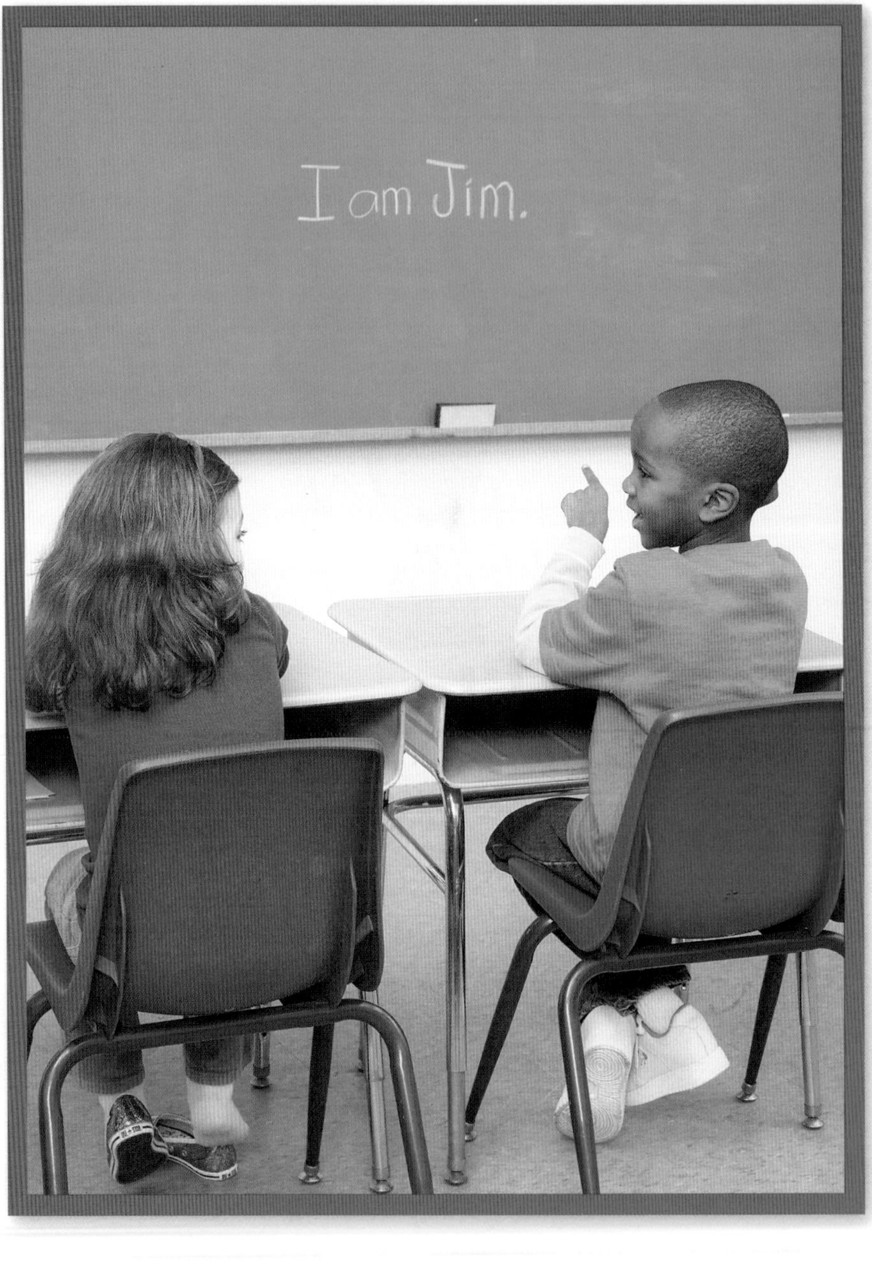

I can read this sentence.

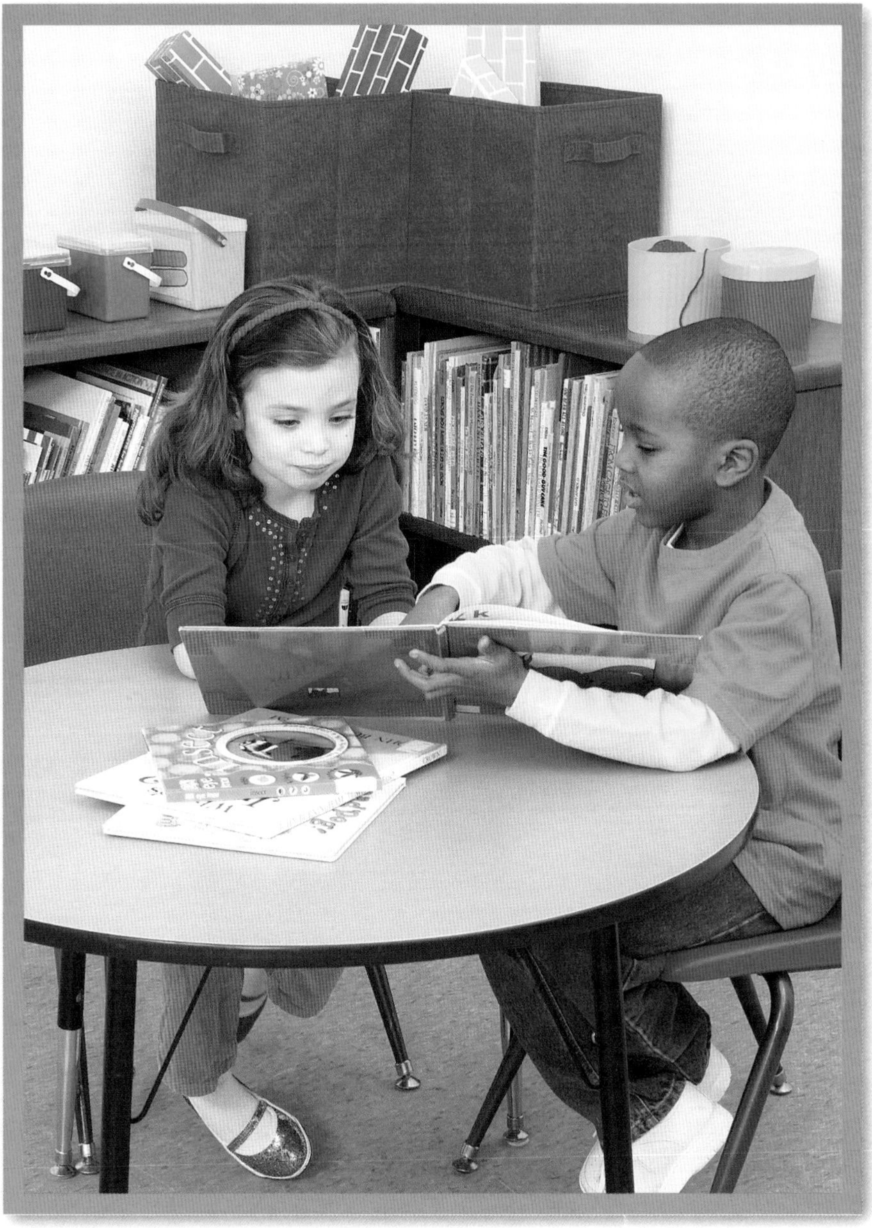

I can read this page.

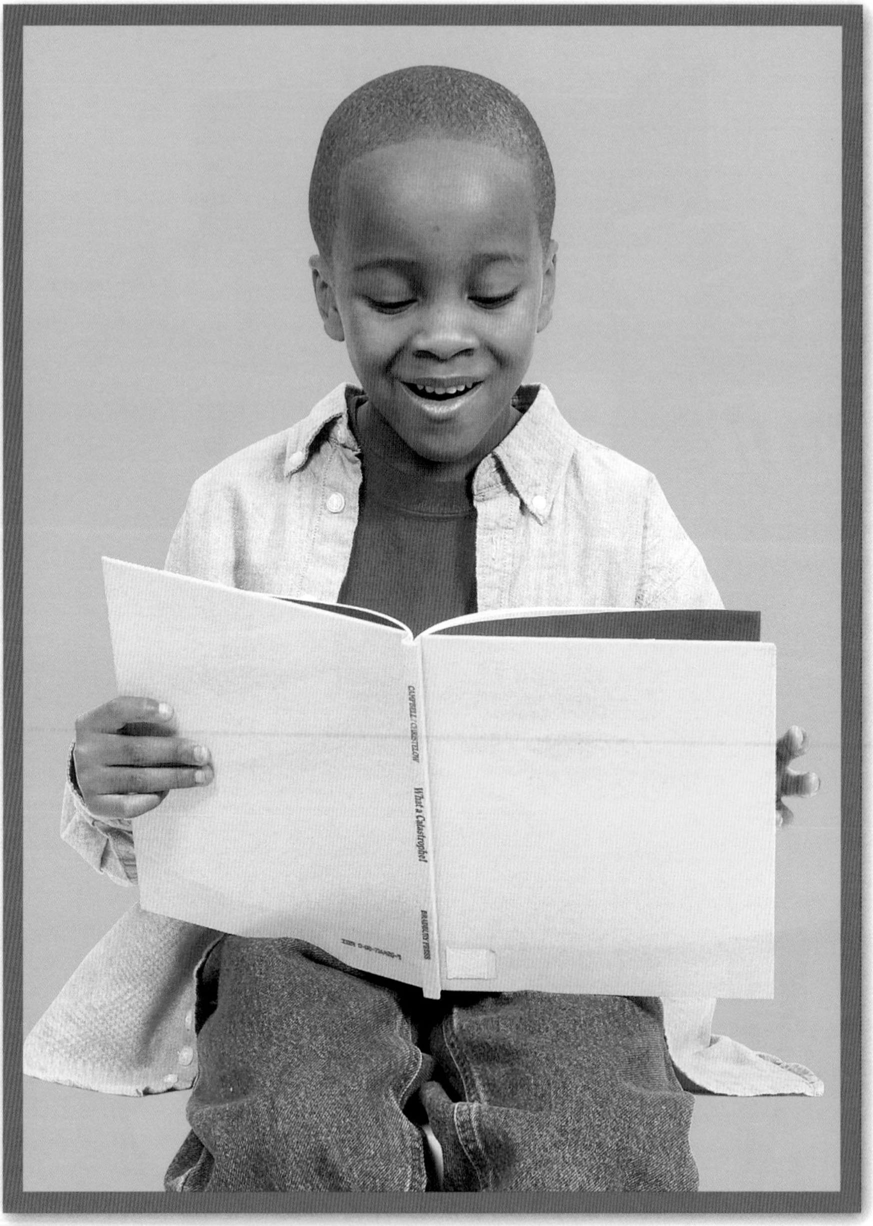

I can read this book!